Under Foot

Under Foot

Poems & Essays

Stephen Lewandowski

Mayapple Press 2014

Published by   MAYAPPLE PRESS
362 Chestnut Hill Rd.
Woodstock, NY 12498
www.mayapplepress.com

ISBN 978-1-936419-32-6
Library of Congress Control Number: 2013957217

ACKNOWLEDGMENTS

The author thanks the editors of these publications which published poems and essays appearing in *Under Foot*.

Bellowing Ark—Estate Sale, Giant, Hidden, Team Bus
Blue Line—Fit & Form
Connecticut River Review—Naming the Ghost
Convergence—The Hat
Country Journal—Glacial Till, The Hat
Focus on Farming—Fit & Form, The Hat
Greenfield Review—Rainy Day & Full House, Fit & Form
Hanging Loose—Bishop Preserve, Flock of Gulls in a Plowed Field
House Organ—Glare
Lake Country Crafts Journal—Fit & Form
Lake Effect—Niche
Longhouse—Small Town, Small Business, The Hat
Margarine Maypole Orangutan Express—Niche
Mid-America Poetry Review—Ghost Orchard
Outdoor Communicator—Small Town, Small Business, Francis Van OpDorp
Pegasus—The Load
River Poets Journal—Bedrock
Rootdrinker—When You'd See, Second Hand, Big Stones
The Scream—Chip/Block, Infernal
Tellus—Rainy Day & Full House
The Trumpeter—The Soil Scientist Digs a Hole
Upstream—Late Nap
Wild Earth—Bare and South Hills
Written on Water anthology—Small Town, Small Business

Cover art "Long Pond," painted by Seth C Jones; from the collection of Judith Kerman. Cover designed by Judith Kerman. Book designed and typeset by Amee Schmidt with titles and text in Perpetua. Author photo courtesy of Ray Lindquist.

Contents

Listening Landscape   3

My Name   4

Ghost Orchard   5

Summ(on)ing Up My Job   6

Scavengers   7

Summer Job   8

Agricultural Stabilization and Conservation Service   9

Francis Van OpDorp   10

Journal, July 15, 1978   11

Jeff   12

Bishop Preserve   14

On Bare Hill   15

When You'd See   16

Casey   17

Small Town, Small Business   18

The Load   19

Glacial Till   20

Bedrock   21

Blasters   23

Destroying Angel   24

Niche   25

Naming the Ghost   26

Leland's Mines   30

Lines Written Before an Autumn Dawn   32

Team Bus   33

Estate Sale   34

Heavy   35

Flock of Gulls in a Plowed Field   37

Late Nap   38

Some People   39

Inevitable   40

Infernal   42

Glare: Full Moon on the Equinox   43

Unsaid   44

Rhoda's Song   45

Gesture   47

Morning at the Nursing Home   48

Sacred Hill   49

Homing   50

Instructions   51

Fulfillment: Further Instructions   52

Detox Among the Shades   53

Easy   55

The Hat   56

Fossil Hunting   57

Chip, Block   60

Rainy Day & Full House   61

Hidden   62

Fit & Form   63

The Soil Scientist Digs a Hole   64

Bare and South Hills   65

Second Hand   66

Frugality   68

Requiem   70

Big Stones   71

Listening Landscape

The new antenna for
the old all jazz all the time
nonprofit radio station
reaches deep into
the hills & valleys
south of the city so
now we can have
Oscar Peterson flowing
with our morning coffee

Presumably Oscar's piano
travels on to
near-infinity across
the Great Lake to the north
waves of music lapping at
the pre-Cambrian Shield

Driving, I lose the music
pressed against the hill's flank
while across the narrow valley
sunlight threads the gap
and flashes off brilliant
maple leaves drifting over
soil horizons of
the abandoned gravel pit

Driving & rising into the
sound of familiar voices
waves washing the air but
detained by the hillside
falling into the valley's silence
most profound where the road
is pinched by the woods
a shade falling from
overhead even at noon

My Name

is long on the lips and heavy
on the tongue, I've carried it
these years as best I can
since my father gave it to me.
It is common in Poland's
mouth and on the south sides
of Chicago and Buffalo.
My mother's family hated
the name, putting me in a pickle.

How many times
have I spelled it out?
Those listening frown
as if it cost them something.
Only once did someone say,
"That's a lovely name," and
only Marvin insisted on
pronouncing it correctly.

But then I come from a country
of long names, some of them
in language not foreign at all—
Canandaigua, Tonawanda,
Cattaraugus, Ganondagan—
just sound it out.

Ghost Orchard

What once was
in living memory
eight acres of Black Cherry
or *Prunus avium* orchard
bearing heavily while tended
by Old Man Woodward
over the years has been
parceled out and built up
with modest houses in
styles of the time, but
at this time of year
every year, the surviving
black straggles of
cherry limbs and bark
though uncared for
maimed and broken
suddenly burst forth
in sprays and fountains
of white blossoms

Summ(on)ing Up My Job

The outfits I worked for
had long names adding
to the local alphabet soup
but accurately describing
their functions.
When I answered the phone
I'd shorten them up
to a few key words.
After I said, "Soil Conservation,"
sometimes there'd be a pause
followed by a querulous voice—
it must have been the fault
of my awful upstate accent—
they'd ask, "Soul Conservation?"
Then, perversely, I'd say, "Yes,
who were you calling for?"

Scavengers

gang of crows
floats up, then flees
noisily down-wind
from the top of
a big-tooth aspen
whose branches
have snared
a frail scrap of
the day-time moon

Summer Job

For Barbara McClintock

Counting blue
leafhoppers
in the whorl
of a corn leaf

Before & after
application

Still staring down
into the green vortex

Agricultural Stabilization and Conservation Service

Rain on & off
all day long
the last day
to certify fields
for set-aside programs
farmers file in
joking & scuffing
the rug, jostling
rows of metal
filing cabinets

Francis Van OpDorp

(1934—2006)

There's a stone
in the middle of this hill.
I know because
I helped to put it there.
The road used to curve around it,
going this way past.
But when we moved here in '46
I was just a boy
we dug a hole
right alongside
worked the stone loose
and dumped it in
covered it over.
Now you see, in this field
we got even rows and
the road goes straight past.

Journal, July 15, 1978

The rolling field lies like an outstretched hand, palm up. Ridges and valleys proceed north and south, the broad palm is almost flat land engraved with plowed swirls. A red-tailed hawk soars over the southeast corner and drops a feather which I'll find later. Where the thumb would be, two workers in silver hard hats drill for water for a planned house. Their rig rocks like a clumsy but obstinate dinosaur, roaring gas engine driving the star bit through bedrock.

Bill and I work in another part of the field, walking the spaces between the fingers to measure and survey for drainage pipes. Behind us we leave a trail of bright orange flags. The machine furnishes us a rhythm for work, and the drillers watch us trudge around whenever they can look away from their rig.

A house once stood where we walk. All gone now except for a few broken bricks and a plot of dark earth on one hill. The freshly plowed earth shows specks of broken china and glass. Fragments of a cobalt blue porcelain cup, a green glass bottle with bubbles, and a plate with a walled and towered city print surface. A light rain washes them clean. I slip my finger through the broken-off handle of a redware jug. Figures cross a bridge beneath weeping willows as a lark soars above. Hands and mouths touched and washed. From the kitchen hearth, the meal comes to a table set with linen and silver in the dining room, and the house glows for a moment with warmth, light and music.

Clods of red clay soil moistened by the rain cling to my boots. The surveyor runs out of notebook paper—the truck with supplies is a long way off—and he writes the figures down in ballpoint on his palm. For the rest of the day he walks around with the transit slung over his shoulder and a column of numbers kept on his hand.

Jeff

The first time I met Jeff, he was on his feet yelling at me over the heads of a roomful of seated people. "If you want our land, you'll have to pay for it," he shouted. I had just finished giving a talk on protecting the lake by protecting its watershed to a full house, saying, "How we treat land will determine the quality of our water resources." Jeff's face was red and he was yelling because he didn't like what he was hearing.

Younger, Jeff had farmed for a living. Then, because he was good with equipment, he picked up some work digging ditches and repairing septic systems in the suburbs. Later, he farmed around the edges of subdivisions, renting land cheap. Increasingly, he dug foundation holes and septic trenches, but once the house was built, there was no more farming that land.

Little by little he worked himself out of farming. When the land he owned became so valuable for development that he could hardly pay the taxes from what he raised on it, he sold it off and moved away from the suburbs, down into our neck of the woods.

That's when I met him, shouting at me from the back of a crowded room that my kind of talk was exactly what drove farmers off their land. He'd heard it before. I was going to tell him how to farm! He waved his big red hands in the air, making his point. He had come in late, wouldn't sit down, and stood in back with several other late-comers waiting for a chance to let us all know how he felt. The crowd craned their necks to see what all the noise was about.

Several years later, when a watershed agricultural committee was formed, a Town Supervisor asked Jeff if he would serve. My job was to advise that committee. Jeff accepted the invitation and became an outspoken committee member. When Jeff had something on his mind, no matter who was involved, he would speak up. He asked questions in ways that couldn't be ignored. Even if another farmer disagreed with him and thought he was all wet, he'd have to answer Jeff's questions.

At a committee meeting one night, Jeff told a story on himself. He'd been on the committee for more than a year, and he started by making several comments about what he'd thought of the watershed program when he first came on board. His mildest remark was that he'd thought it a waste of time.

Then he began his story, "You know when you're in a hurry, sometimes things happen." Everybody nodded. Earlier that week, he and a hired man were plowing and disking a field for winter wheat. They'd heard that some rain was due that night, so they were in a hurry to get the ground worked up and planted. The tractor the hired man was driving was heating up, and Jeff knew that it needed an oil change. Because they were in a hurry, they didn't go back to the barn but brought the filter and oil right out into the field. The hired man stopped the tractor, got down, pulled the plug and started to drain the oil. Jeff saw that the oil was running out of the engine right onto the ground. Though he would have thought nothing of it in the past, suddenly he heard himself say, "Hey, don't do that! Don't you know we're in a watershed?"

Bishop Preserve

in Fayette, New York

His labor
to set nature in place
works easily, constantly
covering the ground

Trusty Volvo station wagon
parked in what was a clearing
pines planted all around
engulf the car over years
with branches & needles
cones, scales, drips of sap
it becomes almost
another White Pine

The mice ride to heaven on
an engine compartment stuffed
with walnuts, trunkful of seeds
fuzzy nests burrowed in the backseat
the car sinks up to its hubs in the duff
pines race toward the sun

It seems like only
a moment ago
he was called away

On Bare Hill

Hard to find footing
by frozen pools
that will be vernal
in months to come

Red Cedar plumes
sprout and re-sprout
damaged by wind
and deer browse

their needles sharp enough
to prick even a callused thumb
crushing it for scent

where the west wind
tore out the lead
the tree forms a cup,
an uplifted crown

a bed in which
a body could be held
soul floating upward
from your branches

the summit ground by ice
swept hard and weathered
snow drifting in the lee
clouds streaming over

When You'd See

Our friend Craig around town
right away you'd notice
his short arms. He was a short
guy anyway but his arms
were really short. Bustling
down the street, he'd always
carry a pack of tickets
in his breast pocket—
to get you into the Trooper's Club,
a chance at the Rotary 50-50, or
the Hatch Hose Lucky Number.
He'd stop to talk, "Hey, how's it going?"
and you'd be looking away
from those tickets, but couldn't—
I'd try to figure out what great luck
and chance of a lifetime had just
passed me by, but I'd never ask.
"See you later." You see
once you asked, he had you.
Now that Craig is gone, I wonder,
Did he think I was kind of a stiff?

Casey

You've probably heard of jackknife carpenters, but I was a jackknife fisherman. That means, you see, that I didn't do things strictly legal. I always kept my knife open, right next to me on the seat.

One night I was out fishing in a small boat. Didn't have but one seat in it, little thing. I thought I heard something, looked up and around, tilted the lantern this way and that. But I couldn't see a thing and went back to my fishing. I was fishing with treble gang hooks—you'd put a minnow on the top ones and hope that the fish would snag themselves on the lower when they bit. They was illegal, of course, because you was allowed only 30 hooks in those days, and that gave me 60, see. I was fishing with my jackknife open, right there on the seat beside me.

One moment it was quiet, and the next the game warden, his name was Jack White, jumped right into my boat! Almost dunked us both. He'd rowed up quiet in back of me in the dark. Well, I'll be damned! Didn't have time to do nothing—there he was, big as life. He kind of hunched down on the gunnel of that little boat and said, "Casey, reel in, I want to see your rig."

He thought he had me. I was stalling for time, and I says, "Can't you wait a minute, Whitey? I think I got a bite." When I'd said that, my hand went for the knife, and *whisht*, the line was cut and my kit was overboard and headed for the bottom of the lake. Well, he was pretty mad at that, and we sat there on the lake and had a long discussion of course. During the discussion, his boat floated off into the dark.

After a while he saw he wasn't going to get anywhere arguing with me, so he said, "Casey, row me back to my boat." "The hell I will, mister!" I said, "I just decided to fish the other side of the lake. And with that I pulled up anchor and started rowing for the other side, with him holding for dear life, and us arguing, and the boat almost shipping water all the way across.

Pretty soon we came up on High Banks on the other side, just a little bit of beach there, cliffs straight up from the water and no road within a mile. I rowed right ashore, stepped out on the beach, grabbed the bow of the boat and tipped it up. He cursed and fell over backwards off the stern into the water. I guess you could say he was mad. Never did know how he got home.

Small Town, Small Business

Claude McWilliams, of
the McWilliams Agency
Insurance and Real Estate
wears his usual outfit—
white shirt, suspenders
and bow tie—as he grubs
with the heel of his shoe
at grass growing through
cracks in the sidewalk
before his place of business.

The Load

The piece was damned heavy
and lay flat on the floor.
Sonny and I decided
to lift it together.
We bent down, got a hold
and slowly tipped it up.
It was so heavy I saw stars.
I said to Sonny, "I see stars."
"Yeah I know, he said,
"I see your stars too."

Glacial Till

Rocks are signed
with a signature
of great stress,
patience's secret name.

Stone eggs nest
in the loam.

Silt, clay, sand
gravel, cobble, boulder.

Milky Way lights spread
across the freshly cracked
center of a cobble of gneiss.

This stone seems
decorated
with garnet studs.

How deep can you see
into the quartz pebble?

Limestone lozenge,
glacial worrystone
has been smoothed, then
engraved with a picture:
electrons streaking across
a cloud chamber photograph.

The farmer jokes that
his best crop is rocks.
Picks them fresh each spring.

Information put away
for a new Stone Age:
Flint fractures clean &
can be flaked to a sharp
& useful edge.

Bedrock

Laid down layer by
layer of sediment
eroded from the landmass
and raining onto seabed over
whole colonies of Fenestella and Polypora
Neospirifera and Rhipidomella
shapes impressed in the mud shower

hills thrust above the water
and set on edge
their weak places washed away,
joints eroding and scattered
pressure heaving them higher
even as they wear down

ground by great icesheets
advance and retreat
gobs of sediment adhering
to the glacier's sole and
scouring the exposed bedrock
high places made low again

chunks cracked out of
the bed by frost, tumbling
down a bank from the gully
hidden in hemlock growth
and washed with the stream
flow of mud, stone, debris

settling into
an alluvium
a hayfield
where we sit for a music festival
afternoon stretching into the evening
the stones are hard
on our comfort, no place
to take it easy without

a point in your rib or hip
so a prize is offered
for the best stone sculpture

dancing couples and groups
a twirling solo
some take a break to
comb the site
for materials

300 million year old stone
washed and ground under the sole
of a glacier
a child picks up one, then another,
examines them closely
for a hidden shape
then makes the form of a hawk
castle turtle rocket bear

Blasters

When LaVerne bought the farm, he wondered why one field was never drained. In a dry year, you might get some decent corn, but usually everything drowned out. When he looked, he found a stone the size of this room buried in the way. Blaster drilled six feet through granite to set the charge. Explosions threw shards all over the field, their raw surface striking with blood red garnet crystals.

Old Sam would lay a little dab of mud on the stone, set his charge, fire it off, then wheel the trencher right back in and peel off the shattered rock layers. After a while, same thing all over again.

Hired another fella once, laziest man you ever saw, but he knew his blasting. He sat on the tailgate of his truck, smoking. He'd bundle the charge, attach the fuse, then loan you his cigar to light it. Running as fast as you could, rocks as big as your two fists together would fall on you. Some of us hid under the wagon. Rocks hit the clay tile piled on the wagon and broke a lot.

Standing joke is that a blasted ditch is best—no spoil to spread.

Destroying Angel

Krieger says *virosa* is
the most poisonous
of the *Amanita* tribe,
but to stay safe
one need only
avoid eating it.
Not so easy to avoid
when the angel is beautiful,
lightly dressed and only
wants to be touched.

You see, abstention
was never an option
from when she arrived
carrying two ice cream
sundaes melting
the fudge dripping
down sticky containers.
"Would you like one?"
There weren't enough
napkins to contain
that flood.

Like other men
I could only
blush and lick my fingers
that was some dessert
only later the poison began
to work on my innards
and by then it was too late
to simply throw it up.

Niche

Every fall,
the County Highway Department
deposits, truck by truck,
a huge pile of sand & gravel—
corner of the Bloomfield &
Ionia Roads. All winter,
behind it, the young
Deputy Sheriffs
hide.

Naming the Ghost

For Jim La Villa-Havelin

It is rumored that walking down a New World
village lane one day in the sixteenth century,
a *grenouille*, I mean a Frenchman, looked askance
and, nudging his buddy, shouted, "*Quel hure!*"
while goggling at a strolling male warrior.

The "*hure*" might have called himself *wyandot*
if he answered such rudeness in words,
or he might have preferred to let
his big hickory club do the talking.
The periwigged *francais* compared
the *huron's* hairstyle to a bristly boar.

Our woodchuck is also an unkempt
New World fellow but could not be
confused with the swaggering *huron* dude
sporting roaches, bangles, earrings, scalp lock,
a "walking" stick and tattoo
of a man smoking the moon.
The bright silver brooches
pinned to his scarlet broadcloth coat
were the very height of fashion.

*

When, a hundred years later,
the Church of England snobs ridiculed
nonconformists as *enthusiasts*,
they sneered at their praying antics
in the sanctuary where the juju really took hold.
Besides, said the elite, they are so *plain.*

The Friends reacted to their words
by waiting in silence, foreswearing swearing,
dressing in undyed sack and calling
themselves not Friends but those

whose spirit Quaked before the Lord.
We *will not* take off our hats!

For a week in September, 1779, colonial troops
were commanded to destroy
the Iroquois' *Kendaia* village.
First, they admired the homes as better built
and with more window glass than their own
and sheltered in them while they burned
stored corn & beans, chopped down
apple & peach orchards, then torched the homes.
Total destruction is hard work when you only
have axes and fire and need to keep looking
over your shoulder the whole time.

*

After the war-time boom,
Sampson Air Force Base departed
Kendaia in the late 1950s leaving
a string of busted garages and diners
and depot bunkers full of nuclear
weapons waste.

When land for Sampson was seized on a month's
notice from local farm families in July, 1942
they say they felt like dogs turned out of their own homes
and still remember their ruined gardens years later.
Those who stayed suffered a living death
haunting their own woods and fields.

*

White as my face is, it would take a lot
of my nerve to call anyone "spook,"
but once I knew a true spook
who operated Kabuki-style
traveling the world in the submarines
of Naval Intelligence. One of his
best disguises was a trim mustache
on the smiling face of a slight, neat man.

You should have seen him in whites!
His charm turned the whole ship upside
down when he dressed as a woman.
Pressured to confess, his spirit tried to
escape by driving the family station wagon
loaded with gallons of bright paint
—no skid or swerve—
into a bridge abutment.

*

Not much remains of Sampson's playing fields
or that weathered sign painted on the back
of the backstop—outline of the horsehide
mandala with symmetrical stitching painted
along the seams and BASEBALL writ large
across its center—where the flyboys used
to play the townies. The pitcher's mound &
basepaths are gone but shape of the infield
and outfield diamonds remain though lately
plowed and now planted to winter wheat, rows of
green spikes coming up through the snow.

*

Instant destruction haunts the world
dressed in the raiment of
fear and self-loathing.
The power "unleashed" cannot
be collared or contained
or brought to heel.
Hiroshima's shadows are permanent
shades etched in concrete.
The sacred technicians assembling
bombs christen them improbably
Little Boy, Fat Man, and Thin Man
as if personae in a morality play except
the good and evil characters become
so entwined we can't tell the
difference, if there ever was one.

Giant

Sugar maple
branches reaching
skyward, roots
sucking the earth
to create in time
a huge fissured trunk

To be a giant
one only need grow
large enough
to shelter others

When a branch breaks and
blows away in the wind
a sweet substance
pours from the wound

As we walk by, we admire
the shade but fear
the weight of years'
growth hanging
over our heads

You hold
this place together
heaven & earth,
light & dark and
now, now, now
guard the gate
life & death

Leland's Mines

Leland Crow pops out of the health food section of the megamarket as I walk by. He greets me cheerily, "Hey Steve, how's the book coming?" I'm glad to see him too. Of all the people I've told about my book project, he has been most faithful in asking about its progress when we meet. Of course, the subject of the book has changed over the years so we are now discussing an idea three or four generations removed from the original. But that doesn't matter to Leland—to him, a book's a book.

I ask what he's doing here, the last place I would expect to see him, being the picture of health at his age and an unlikely purchaser of vitamins or other supplements. Perhaps he's here on behalf of someone else or has wandered over while his wife browses the produce.

He says he's looking for an extract of horse chestnuts, something good for varicose veins. He asks if I suffer from varicose veins. When I say no, he expresses relief because "They hurt like hell sometimes, you know." Leland has always lived an active life, and I am surprised to hear that anything might slow him up. He is dressed in a full suit of grey cotton work clothes, old ones, not new. Pictures of Leland from way back show his longish red hair combed straight back, and now and then you'll see that red hair come out in his temperament. But usually he is as mild as his grey hair, now cut short.

"It's funny to meet you here," I say, meaning the health food section of a market that offers food from all over the world for sale. Leland has worked all his life as an operator of heavy equipment and owns quite a collection of machines rusting in his side yard. I met him first when he was called on to excavate a pond, and I was logging the test pits.

Later, in semi-retirement, except when one of his boys or friends would call him out to run a machine or drive a truck, he presided over a gentleman's coffee-klatch of five or six at the Company Store where I'd stop each morning for coffee and a newspaper. We always talked, and he would send me off each morning with "Be careful out there."

I say, "I was just working on something for the book and walked over for a cup of coffee. Sometimes I think better when I walk."

"What's that book about again?" he asks.

I say it's a sort of natural history of this area.

He asks, "Will it include something about the Indian silver mines over by Seneca Lake?"

"No," I say, thinking that I'd never heard that one before, "It's more about what we'd eat if we ate just what came from this land." I avoid the word "cuisine" from the essay's title because I think it might sound too fancy to him.

"That's a good thing to write about," he says, unconcerned about my lack of information about the silver mines but always glad to talk about food.

I ask after his health. He says, "Not bad for an old fella but of course I take on too much. Planted too big a garden, then took on a couple excavating jobs when I know I shouldn't. But I played too much as a young man and now I have to pay, you know, work longer."

"Silver mines," I think, walking away. Where does that come from? Then I remember Joseph Smith, the Mormon founder who was also a treasure digger. Surely he too was searching for the openings of ancient silver mines beside Seneca Lake a hundred and fifty years ago. Smith dug his golden plates out of the earth near Palmyra then moved on, but ideas about the treasures buried in our hills persist.

Lines Written Before an Autumn Dawn

Yellow the leaves of my
Poems of Wang Wei
cheap paperback
translated by an English
veteran of the Far East
priced $1.85 new
thirty-five years ago
but I must have
bought it used

One spring, a thousand years ago
he wrote, "I am sad at this final
whitening of my hair"
most dismayed to find
himself grown old in
the spring of a new year

Who was the young man
pausing to read these lines
and who now
bends over the page?

Team Bus

For Jay Uhl

Fifty years ago this season
because my uncle was their driver
the boy I was rode the team bus to
high school football games in muddy fields
leaving in daylight and
coming back after dark.
I did not take up a seat but
crouched on the big box heater
beside the driver's seat facing back
and in his care. They were mostly quiet
these movable barns with
herds of young men going out
to batter others and return
in victory or defeat without
much to say either way.
I would hear the coaches afterward
curse their inability to learn
or praise their dumb courage.
It was some time before
I had to learn the physical
courage or mental reserve
of men in teams pulling
toward a common goal, then
sitting in the dim bus with
the stink of their effort,
dirty uniforms covering injuries,
bloody bandages and layers of tape.

Estate Sale

A small estate but sufficient
to the man whose wife died long ago,
and he lived on in the same place
with one room "just as she left it"
full of a lady's pretty things—
a mirrored dresser lined with cosmetics
and a closet full of pastel frocks.
The cupboards have been emptied
of her frilly carnival glass and
blue milkglass salt and pepper set,
nothing he would have used.
"Is there anything up there?"
"No, we brought everything down
from the attic so you can see it."
What was the family name?
"Claus," she says pronouncing it
kloss as in loss, the diphthong
lost and gone a long time.
The 96 year old man's small house
has tool hangers in the mud room,
barns out back and a big garden.
He hung a framed certificate from
Future Farmers of America
on the wall, and there's a prize
bull statuette on his desk.
In his life he managed both
a market in town and a farm that
slowly became the big garden
you could see from the road.
"He was kneeling down
in the dirt planting onions.
The people passing by called
to say they had seen him
lying on the ground, and
that's how we found him."

Heavy

The dump truck and flatbed
trailer have no escort
their tailgate proclaims a
WIDE LOAD trundling
down the highway
loaded on the flatbed—
its tracks caked with mud,
arm fully extended and
exposed piston spotless,
two-yard bucket yawning
not clean but empty—
the chained machine curls
into a fetal position
much like sleep, rests
a Samsung backhoe
the load is bound
for another project where
the roused backhoe will snort
diesel smoke and reach
to take a big bite out
of the landscape

                *

I'm following BOMAG
down the road, slow
steel drum on pavement
rings like a chime
the roller's name is stamped
in bold yellow capitals
across its rear end
lined up perfectly
with my windshield
big guy operating
the machine
never looks back
takes one hand

off the wheel
pulls off his cap
to rub his head
scratch his hair
must feel pretty good—
all that slow mo down below
traffic tagging along behind
in a little parade

Flock of Gulls in a Plowed Field

We know they fell
from the heavens, but
they arrange themselves
to resemble scraps of wrapping
torn from some previous world
like snow sealing the ground
and surviving in hedgerow's shade.
The cover has been pulled back
and plowed in to release
the field's breath as a mist.

The mist carries
exhalations of sightless
soil flora & fauna.
The flock patrols the field
looking closely for signs of food
while casting a careful eye over
other traffic, safe as long as it flows.

Each day the earth is a present
newly arriving, given to creatures.
Each day they tear the wrapping
away from the wound
and begin to feed.

Late Nap

For Chip Schramm (1947-2004)

In a jumble of winter lateness—
of day, light and life—
he lay down on the white blanket
covering her bed where she joined him.
His eyes shut, opened, then shut
and stayed closed while
outside the northering sun
turned white sheets covering fields
to scraps left in the shade and
decayed drifts in the hedgerows.

While he slept, she touched his arm,
hip, neck, and smiled when he woke
to find her watching him sleep.
In the late winter afternoon,
darkness rose to the precise level
of his eyes as his eyelids fell
until they touched her face.

Some People

For LaRoy Benham Sterling (1906-1984)

Drink, others watch
day-time television,
navigating the soaps
from a barcalounger in
their deceased parents' homes.
Some like Butch do both and
punctuate the day's grey
and the screen's blue light
with a glowing cigarette.
He watched the family plumbing
business peter away, not feeling
up to answering the phone.

Then, he would take some
time off from his regimen
and repair to the shadowy
bar of the Green Front tavern
to drink in the silent
company of others ranged
before the beer advertisement's
everflowing waterfall.
They lift an elbow to sacrifice
a long-necked Bud or Genny
to their work-suited reflection
in the ornate mirror behind the bar.

Perhaps it would have been better
if he, LaRoy, had never been born,
but now, as Butch, he had
to see it through to the end.

Inevitable

He coined each canto
as if it were cash
to be tried between
the teeth and discovered
much too late after seeing
"petals on a wet, black bough"
it was all metaphor.

His father worked
at the mint pressing
U.S. dollars and cents,
his own name
a standard measure
of weight and currency,
attended a college
named for Hamilton,
inventor of American banks,
and became a money-nut
spewing hate on those who
controlled the currency
and let money for gain.
Captured, he was caged
and pressured to confess
his counterfeit thoughts
but produced instead
"what thou lovest well remains."

*

Poets deal so heavily
in metaphor & symbol that
they may mistake the actual
for the virtual or is it really
like the chestnut that
"the best manure is the farmer's footprint"
with the farmer epitomized
by footprints farming better

than the farmer who leaves none, not
even symbolically present on the farm.
The truth is that in cloddy soil
seeds will sprout first & best
in ground pounded by the farmer's boots.

    *

In my garden's clumpy soil
worked too soon or too wet
after planting by hand a block
of ten rows of sweet corn,
my boots walk heel to toe
along the rows treading
corn kernels into the dust
so that—come rain—
everything is "satisfactual."

Infernal

My hands grip the wheel
can we drive to hell or will
we have to get out and walk?
Did I make a wrong turn?
I thought I knew
where this road goes
then the walls close in
the tunnel narrows so
there's no turning around
or backing up
I can only go ahead
into the dark
my lights don't seem
to be working right—no
beam from high or low
on the tunnel walls
I must be heading
for rebirth or digestion
does the car have a soul?
where will I park?

Glare: Full Moon on the Equinox

Like uneasy mushrooms, insecurity
light fixtures sprout
from our buildings & parking lots.
Fear of the dark is contagious.

A dim corner back of the convenience
store where teens used to park
is now fiercely lit.
Between the house and barn
innocuous moths pursued
by bats throw great shadows.

The moon disdains
such displays and withdraws
behind a cover of clouds
where Mars attends her.

Even the once-dark fields just shorn
of their corn, where owls & foxes
used to hunt, are so bright that
the mice are scared of their shadows.
An unseen galaxy whispers,
"You are wasting your light."

Unsaid

As usual between friends
we pass back & forth
stories our lives present us with
they might be true
but between you & me
for some questions, the most
elegant answer is silence

We walked out from your kitchen
into the presence of tombstones
whose granite fairly glows
in the moonlight

When you ask,
"How is that word spelled
for those little people
those stone-throwers,
those pumpkin rollers?"
I can't tell you
what silence
comes over me
"I don't even know
what you're talking about."

Rhoda's Song

The shady, twisting trail
winds as the creek bends
forced to follow
through a floodplain
laced with abandoned channels
covered with white toothwort and
studded with massive sycamores,
overspreading black walnuts
willows & cottonwoods whose
mass is less striking because
they grow so rank

In the village, David was on a ladder
reaching up to paint
his white house even whiter
when he turned to my greeting
the sun was in his eyes
he said, "Who is that?" and
I said, "Stretch," the name
he was once known by

I reminded him of a story
of his father who was, like David,
the Village Attorney, and
he re-told the story, mending my errors,
which ends with a gesture: index finger
held vertical against his lips for *sshhh*

Walking the trail into town
reminds me of David's mother
Rhoda a real lady who died on the trail
out for her early morning walk alone
and lay there until frozen to the ground
and found by a passerby

Just as the length of the trail is in
the shade of these great trees

you are seldom out of
earshot of its water's voice
whether running low over summer stones
or as Rhoda must have heard that cold day
a simple melody of repeated tones as
the water clanks and rings against ice

Gesture

No time
for niceties—
we plant trees
in the wet ground
between showers.
Shovel blade slices
sod under my foot,
you jam fine roots,
fold and stamp until
the mud mouth closes.
Reach again and
pull to be sure
then move on.

Morning at the Nursing Home

In the closed air there is the smell of
food that she has rejected for days

someone shuffles past in a
housecoat and slippers, pushing
a walker like a plow

she has not risen for weeks
and reclines in a hospital bed
head elevated and surrounded
by clean white linens, her face
on the pillow turned to the wall

her breathing labors as it has for days
sometimes pausing a few beats
before going on, her mouth
so slack she can no longer
swallow food, drink or medicine

they tell us she hears us profess
our love when they place
a morsel of ease
under her tongue

Sacred Hill

Needn't be large but
when you go by
you should feel
your heart reaching out
to the place

Like this mound

Corn rows
cobbles
hedgerow
nothing unusual in
a swell of land
but it says
Rest here a while

Homing

Flint, New York

the wide spot now barely a hamlet
but still standing at the intersection
of vectors of power, wealth and influence
forming an asterisk

oldest and most deeply incised
is tree-lined Flint Creek,
sweeping down from the wooded hills
of Italy and Jerusalem, bound
north toward Oswego and Ontario

the second flow is the ancient
east-west trail paced a foot deep
by the Iroquois but
now paved and occupied by
several lanes of traffic on
the way Albany & Buffalo

the third flow flies above the traffic
branch of the Pennsy RR
heavy cast iron bridge on
stacked cut stone piers
lately reverted to trail

the place itself some joker
once called Carborundum
meaning *hard* but after
spelling failed many times
reverted to strike-a-light
flint nodules of sharp fractures
encased in beds of limestone

Instructions

for Peter Black

When I go please
        make sure
                I don't go to
the Dead Poets Home
        Oh no, I don't
                want to go there.

I'd much prefer
        to land among
                the hydrologists
where all the talk
        concerns the powers
                of water.

Fulfillment: Further Instructions

for Edith Davey

Departures from this life
      used to be marked by
            hollow words spoken loud—

redemption, salvation
      eternal life—
            whistling past the graveyard.

When I go, expect
      empty phrases—
            then silence.

To you who listen,
      learn from history
            fill the emptiness

with joy, be kind
      to animals and each other,
            do better than I did.

Detox Among the Shades

1.
I met John Logan once in a bar.
How many thousand
poets and others could say
the same?
He was Christ-like,
had Jesus been suffered
to live so long, his skull
rising from the shrubbery
like so much open ground
revealed at snow melt.
He taught poetry & poets.
His own poems are now
collected and wholly revealed
returning again to the anger
and anguish he felt—
that father figure
pausing over his glass
barely contained.

2.
John, I will trade you
a story for the pleasure
your work gives.
My home is both shaded
and endangered by
a massive silver maple
with ivy covered bark.
The snowbanks below
are littered with ivy leaves
on days with no wind.
Knots in the tree
have rotted to holes and
in the cavities live
families of starlings
who both lodge in

and eat the ivy stems.
After a cold night
they fly out to greet
the dawn, shitting
with glee on the poet's
nondescript black car
parked beneath, that one with
vivid white and blue-green stripes.

3.
Seriously
(that word must announce
the death of the poem unless)
the poem is already
mortally wounded
by the growth of parentheses
attached and sending roots
to suck sustenance from
the tree's fissures and crevices.
It won't surprise you
John that a poet lives
in the presence of rot
and is bombarded
by shit from above.
Sic semper poeta,
The poem grows from such shit.

Easy

Don't look now don't
turn your head
but death is always
immediately available
no need to travel
to some distant land
it's close at hand
homegrown—
I've got a little
patch going out back—
a late night swim
in the frigid lake,
a kiss off
the bridge abutment,
dropping into
Ithaca's gorgeous gorges.

The Hat

Old Jim always wore
a suit, tie, white shirt,
and a hat—you'd never
see him without his hat.
He'd visit a job and maybe
see something he didn't like—
why, he'd take off his coat,
roll up his sleeves and
get right up on the dozer
to run it himself.
When he'd get really mad,
he'd snatch off his hat,
throw it on the ground
and jump right on it.
One day, I saw him
fire his best operator.
He visited a job over in Galen
and didn't like the work
his man was doing.
He started to yell,
snatched off his hat
and threw it on the ground,
but before he could jump on it,
the operator did.

Fossil Hunting

fr. the Latin fossilis, *something dug up*
Preserved remains or record of the presence of plants or animals

First impressions can be deceptive. Most of us came to fossils through our interest in dinosaurs and the lush land life of the Jurassic Period. We expect our fossils to be big, dramatic, preferably carnivorous animals. Who wasn't tremendously excited to see the battle between Triceratops and Tyrannosaurus rex in *Fantasia?* So that's what we thought fossils were all about. We were disappointed to learn that our fossils, here in the Finger Lakes, weren't dinosaurs. The Jurassic was relatively recent and short-lived compared to the fossil record of our area. Fossils of this region tend to be small aquatic life forms, such as sponges, corals and bivalves. One rarely runs across a predator. It's hard not to be disenchanted at first.

It so happens that the part of the Devonian Period into which our streams and rivers have carved an entry through cliffs and gullies was extremely rich in life from which fossils could be made. Three hundred sixty million years ago, this area was underwater and going through a sedimentary process in which hard-bodied life forms were buried in the sediments settling out of the water. First, stone formed a cast around their shape, and later their shape was replaced by stone.

Fossil hunting requires exposed bedrock, and bedrock is naturally exposed, even fractured and grooved, where glaciers have been at work. In western New York the glaciers only went out of business about eleven thousand years ago, so the bedrock they bared is still relatively fresh. Over the past two hundred years, however, the open shale, siltstone, and limestone have been quite thoroughly investigated, first by geologists, then by collectors, and finally by residents, especially children. Teaching western New York State children to look for fossils fulfills an important function in cultural as well as natural heritage.

Learning about fossils enables children to develop the reasoning ability they will need to participate in the scientific method of discovery. The disciplines of Taxonomy, Geology, Paleontology, Zoology, Botany, and Evolutionary Biology, among others, are strongly dependent on understanding the fossil record. Teaching children about fossils will not make scientists of them, but it will keep that option open.

*

Waiting for a friend with business in the town bank, I window shop for clothes, fishing tackle, and toys in the evening along Main Street. The winter darkness has fallen quickly and completely as the display windows are lit. I have some company at the toy store: a well-dressed man stares at the dinosaur display of posters, plastic models, balsa replicas, and blow-ups of the great reptiles.

Lit by recessed spotlights, the bulky Brachiosaurs and Diplodocus browse green Astroturf and flee from Coelurus and Tyrannosaurus while the Pterosaurs float above. Labyrinthodonts bask in the ferns beside blue mirror pools on which Plesiosaurs and Icthyosaurs are poised.

Look, there's a flock of young Ankylosaurs. You can tell because their spines haven't grown in yet. They better be careful, and where do you suppose their momma's at? When I was young and the language was growing in me, it developed frills, lobes, crests and bills like these.

I am wondering if he shares my memories of a childhood lost in books, handling fossils, considering blood-splashed illustrations and fascinated by the ancient world of cold-blooded reptile flesh and teeth tearing at one another when under his breath I hear him say "Oh, wow!"

*

Fossils spark imaginations. We say, "What I hold in my hand was once alive and lived its life right here." Hunting for fossils engages an instinctual recognition of patterns—even years later—and we respond to these patterns emotionally. The thrill of finding a fossil stems not only from the sense of discovery since "It was right there all along and I found it," but from a sense of identification, prompting us to ask, "I wonder what its life was like."

For years, the Devonian period appeared to me in shades of grey, silver, white, brown and black, the predominant colors of the local fossil record in stone. This is probably wrong. How would we know what the actual colors were so many million years ago? Pigments don't fossilize. But there certainly would have been a great deal of green in the plant life, and the most likely modern analog to the shallow, salty Devonian seas are the colorful ocean reefs near modern islands and shores. Imagine the drab grey and brown fossils we dig out of the shale in their original hues—violent purples, brilliant greens and extravagant oranges.

There are a number of activities, fossil-hunting among them, which seem to engage a different set of our senses than everyday life does. I suspect that hunting <u>anything</u> engages these senses in recognition of specific patterns. It may be that these abilities are as ancient as the human hunter-gatherer roles.

I had the experience recently of happening on a pile of limestone left over from a construction project and dumped in a field. At first glance, there didn't seem to be anything unusual about it. As I looked more closely at the stone to try to identify the source, at first I couldn't, but then I saw a horn coral fossil protruding from one stone. No sooner had one fossil appeared than, scanning the pile, hundreds of fossils of all kinds emerged. It was the same stone in the same place in the same light, but suddenly my eyes became attuned to the fossil designs. It was almost like looking into the stone.

I've had similar encounters with mushrooms: out in the woods in the fall after a rain, leaves crunching underfoot, looking for mushrooms but really not much going on. Nothing... nothing, until we saw the first, and then as if by magic there seemed to be mushrooms all around. Recognizing the color and pattern of the first mushroom suddenly revealed a whole field of mushrooms.

Whether the quarry is fossils or mushrooms, berries or animals, there's a consistent pattern of being frustrated at first, then clued in, and finally overwhelmed. Native American herbalists often speak of a similar experience when they describe taking properly respectful approaches to gathering medicinal plants. They say the plants reveal themselves at the right time and when the conditions are right to people who are in the proper frame of mind. If any of these factors are off, the plants will remain "invisible" no matter how thorough the search.

There's always the matter of not finding fossils. Will your day be ruined if you find no fossils? Not likely, because there are many worse ways to spend a few hours than in a deep, shady glen with a small stream and perhaps some waterfalls, ferns and mosses. The dappled light streams through green birch boughs. Pick a hot day, because the glen will always be breathing out cool, hemlock-scented air.

Chip, Block

A small fragment semi-detached
from the library waits patiently
on the sunlit portico for
the library's massive doors
to re-open to the morning.

It slowly classifies the Doric
pillars' column and capital
and recognizes the steps
as Onondaga limestone.
Slanting sunlight reveals
dressing marks left in
scores and dimples from
the steam drill and
handwork with a hammer
and fossils from whole reefs
of horn coral emerge from
steps, floor and lintel.

In time the librarian arrives,
unlocks one side of the door,
then motions to
"Wait one moment please,"
while she unfastens a lock,
then swings the heavy
doors back into the dark.

The fragment is anxious
to re-attach electronically
to several other libraries
from around the world who
began writing a *renga* together.

Rainy Day & Full House

45 Holstein cattle in stanchions
10 heifers tethered by themselves
in one corner, 4 dairymen from
3 generations of the Green family,
two conservation agents,
assorted dogs, cats and kittens.
Gathered first in the barn where
chain tracks pull straw & manure
through a concrete channel
toward tractor & honey-wagon.
Over our conversation local radio
plays Linda Ronstadt singing
"It's the right time of the ni-ight
            for making love."
Everybody wears knee-high rubber boots.

Later we move into the milkhouse and
lean against stainless steel tanks.
Discuss the farm's past and future
with these 3 generations, talk ditches,
common acquaintances, small jokes,
how last year's drain tile system
handles long rains like this one.
Grandpa says, "We need rain for the corn
but could've waited 'til the wheat's off."
When we leave it's still raining and
water from the expanse of barn roof
sings in the gutters and washes past
sand piles beneath huge concrete silos
where some child's left toys:
combine, backhoe, bulldozer, dump truck,
tractor with fittings for plowing & planting.

Hidden

A spring surfaces in the mall parking lot
like some trammeled animal
constantly working to break free

Though its wooded hillside was bulldozed
more than fifty years ago
the puddle re-appears each year
in a set of pavement potholes
no matter how many times it's patched
frozen water lifts
the blacktop off like doffing a cap

Traffic tries to evade it when
possible, but it will grab a wheel,
bend a tie rod, bust an axle

In ancient times, the glacier laid
a vein of gravel in among the clays
causing water to rise from the ground
where creatures wore paths through
the woods to the drinking spot
hunters lay at the spring to slake
their thirst and a whole wedding party
pausing in the shade was blessed

Fit & Form

Field of red clay soil
officially designated "Schoharie"
sticks, oh yes, to
machines and hooves
great clods forming on boots
to pant legs, yes in streaks
smears as it climbs
to face and hands.
Plastic and pliant
deceptive soil sometimes
seeming to give way, sometimes
baked hard as stone, but
becomes slick as a mink
with an inch of rain.
Brings all operations to
a sliding, rutting halt.
Turned over in the fall,
it's prone to lumps and clods,
absolutely demands
the "fitting" services
of harrow and crusher.
With heavy equipment
you have to know to the minute
when to get on and off.
Working it demands patience
and skill like that you observe
in the master potter's hands
forming clay up from
the blob on the wheel
into a light and balanced bowl.

The Soil Scientist Digs a Hole

"You can go places with a spade you can't with a backhoe."

He starts it off with his foot, driving the blade deep and wrenching out clods of soil. He wears cotton work pants, easily dirtied and washed, and leather work boots sufficient to protect his ankles. The spade has a long, narrow blade with a curved, sharp bit. He lifts it as high as his shoulder for each short, chopping stroke, coming down hard to split out the blocky peds of soil, laying them in order on the grass beside the hole so that they form the text of his lecture.

His task is a dissection. He brushes away crumbs of soil and peels back a sliver of clay with the sharp blade. It curls away like a wood shaving or a layer of skin. In the exposed bank you see thin layers of red oxide trapped in bands of grey silt. He cuts through horizons, shows us mineralization and the paths of water leaching through the soil, light shapes like prisms in the earth. The violence of his stroke is matched by his calm voice explaining the materials and their actions and origins in local landscapes.

He digs through thousands of years in a few feet of soil, then pauses to catch his breath. While he stands in the hole gazing out over the land, you almost remember silts and clays filtering down through impounded water, the force of water rushing under ice washing sands and gravels into stratified beds, glacial advance and retreat, outwash and deposition, great calves of ice spawned in the drainages. His gaze passes through time and matter.

After a while, you begin to wonder about the importance of these human beings clustered around the hole, all of us looking intently in, or following his gaze out to the landscape, nodding our heads gravely in agreement.

Bare and South Hills

The woman whose head is buried
deep beneath Canandaigua
whose shoulder surfaces at Bare Hill
whose span of waist is Vine Valley
and whose arch of hip
forms South Hill
lies dreaming

She first lay down
in salt seas amid
swaying fronds of
crinoids & eurypterids

The lake laps her side,
glaciers scarcely troubled her sleep

Now she is shrouded by
aeric haplaquepts, clothed
in growths of Red Cedar,
Pinus strobus and popple

Here the Orphan learned that
leaning against a stone
he could listen
to her dreams

You whose villages
dot the landscape,
who have forgotten
to listen to her
breathing, take care
the day may come when
she will wake and walk again

Second Hand

It used to be
we'd know the origins, materials and
makers of things
landing here because
they would be marked.
Every few days
I'd stop to see what new things
had washed up or blown in.

But now who knows
where they came from,
whose hand made them.
Every day a new crop arrives
we need only sift them and
take according to our needs.

I meet my teacher
and his sidekick at
the local diner. I'm mad
and complaining that
"They made me go down
in the basement to be
fingerprinted so
I could substitute.
See—they're still black.
I couldn't get it off."

He says, "Hey, what's wrong with you?
Haven't you learned anything?
Don't you get it? Be patient—
they can't give it away fast enough.
They will bring it to you.
Wait and see."
He told the truth.

Ten thousand years later,
when we're buried again

in the world's material
when all these goods are
splinters, shards and fragments,
the only way they'll know
you existed will be
those fingerprints
retrieved from the basement.

Frugality

for John Rezelman (1919-2012)

There's a house built from fragments of a ride from the amusement park.
When we didn't have anything else to do, we straightened nails.

*

They towed a boat up the lake, beached it at Hunter's, then tore it apart
for building materials. Little by little, they built it into a cottage, and that
accounts for the portholes. Its cockpit became a garden shed. Every fall
we would coat the metal tools with used motor oil and hang them up.

*

Out on the streets, leftover storm windows and storm doors are tossed,
which can be gathered up and made into coldframes to harden young
plants raised inside before setting them out in the garden.

*

A length of garden hose slit along one side makes a nice protective bumper.
I've snapped it over the end of the d-net to protect the fabric where it
grubs along the creek bed. You still get snags and holes, but not so fast.

*

The highway was built over the top of an old path beaten by generations
of foot traffic. Over the path passed walkers and runner, in groups and
solitary: a hunting party, a swift runner with a message, traders with
packs, a war party, and the hesitant steps of a bridegroom approaching
his bride's village.

*

The gas station becomes a pizza parlor. The pizza parlor becomes a flower
shop, a realtor's office and so on.

*

Little by little, we hauled piles of fieldstone from the bean field and set
them up in five courses as a building foundation. We paved the steps going
down to the cellar with the tops of flat ones.

*

There's nothing like a broken piece of spring steel for holding an edge. Put it in a handle and sharpen an edge for a knife.

*

The old feed and grain becomes a consignment antique boutique. The downtown post office becomes an exercise center. The opera house stands empty many years before becoming a photographer's studio. She uses some of the scenery for props.

*

Here's my bouquet straight from the fields. It cost me a sneeze and tickseeds in my socks. Some seasons, it's shadblow or apple. At the end of the year, it's mixed fleabane, New England aster and several sprays of goldenrod.

*

Mike normally picks up good quality roadkill, which explains the spotted fawn in the back of his pick-up. He'll use most everything but the meat in his crafts. It was damaged by the impact and had lain too long dead for the meat to be good. A bunch of young inner city kids are visiting, and because Mike is a teacher, he lets down the tailgate so that they can see the fawn. He says, "She was born in the brush this spring. Just like you, this baby used to follow her mother everywhere." You have to imagine these tiny hooves rigged as clickets at the shins of a dance outfit. She didn't make it across in time this time, but her toes will dance again when the songs begin.

Requiem

"Bony" the excavators call
this soil at the site of a massive
housing development
machines digging & grading
throw up collections of stone—
not a wall or even a pile—
too glacier-smoothed to stack
instead they collect in circles
like the shadow of a pool

Saw my friend Arthur
tonight all dressed up
in his coffin on a trestle
at the funeral parlor, but
a younger man grins from
the display of faded
color photos pinned
near his mounted trophy deer,
turkey, lake and rainbow trout,
his son & daughter now
grown greet the mourners
with "thanks for coming"

That high, pale forehead though
touched up with powder
makes redundant the stone
they will bury him under
at Rose Ridge, yet they will

Perhaps in another ten thousand
years he will also be unearthed
like the stones so carefully
hidden by a passing glacier

Big Stones

> *"Later I came upon a gigantic stone in a heath. I sat down next to it and perceived that it was covered with signs. I recognized lines and paths similar to those that were engraved in the mysterious hand that belonged to the king. Here the wise man of the king had been and had sought to imitate some lines from the tablet of the worlds. And also from the dumb stone the lament spoke with a soundless voice."*
> —*from* "*The Master of Prayer*," *in* Tales of Rabbi Nachman *by Martin Buber*

Though the landscape of this area was smoothed by the glaciers that left ten thousand years ago, and even before their smoothing, which may not be quite the right word for what a mile of ice does to any rough places, it was a landscape of mild hills and valleys with a great lake plain filled with the debris settling out of the still water, all that the previous glacier left behind.

The dominant particle size of this debris would be measured in hundredths and thousandths of a millimeter, silt and clays. But in the landscape there were exceptions, larger stones, rocks and boulders that were picked up elsewhere and carried, only partially digested in the glacial paroxysm, and buried in the new soils or dumped out on the surface.

In more recent years, some of these big stones, termed "erratics" by our geologists, neatly make what we might have thought an adjective into a noun. In some places they litter the landscape, perched like sentinels of the glacial retreat. They also welcomed the oncoming re-establishment of vegetation either from refugia, small areas of native vegetation unscraped by glaciation, or from the droppings of migratory birds, such as the Passenger pigeons, whose "clouds of birds" were capable of speeding the northern advance of species whose seeds were both tasty and only partially digestible.

How big is a big stone or boulder? A few have been found the size of a small room, eight by twelve. More are the size of a car, say a 1963 Volvo, the humped-back one. Many are the size of an armchair or smaller, a breadbox. The smaller ones, encountered in quantity by an excavator, can be irritating. They will break the tooth off a backhoe as easily as a bigger one. They qualify the soil as being "bony" and extend the period of development site preparation beyond days into weeks and months. Separated and stacked aside from the soil piles, they reach the size of cairns, walls or monuments.

Increasingly, big stones play a role in the development of this area. A few are reserved to flank an entry road, like a pair of parentheses. If the stones found during excavation are not large enough to fill this role, stones may be imported. Locally, there are mines to the north on the Onondaga limestone that will blast or drill a piece loose that would fill the bed of your average pickup (example only, not recommended). The limestone splits out along layers, dark when first exposed and then weathering to a creamy grey, and marked with nodules of darker grey or black flints. They are off-season colors, subtle but pretty.

Still the limestones can only match in bulk, not in age or crystalline structure, the erratics which may be derived from far older metamorphic or even igneous stone. Nothing quite matches a big chunk of gneiss studded with garnet crystals for stone-beauty.

Other big stones mark our landscapes: rough granite curbs shaped on three sides and smoothed on one side, dug in deep and mounted end-to-end so their sides define our roadways. And of course there are those gravestones that go to make up the "marble orchards," with at least one side machined to a smoothness in which a message can be carved. Recently a natural gas pipeline was dug northwest to southeast across this county, and, cruising at four feet beneath the surface, it encountered buried erratics that had to be uprooted so that the gas's path might be smooth from Victor to Gorham. These big, smooth tablets and lobes of stone were scraped and clawed out of the ground by a backhoe and laid up beside the trench, later to be hauled away.

A big stone makes a unique memorial for those whose hour of strutting this stage has ended. Dr. Dwight R. Burrell was an "alienist" at various asylums around the country before becoming the head of the Brigham Hall Asylum for the Insane in Canandaigua in 1876. Before he died in 1910, he chose his own monument. For my money, it's both the best and least-worked stone in Woodlawn Cemetery, a four by five by eight foot boulder as headstone with a brass plaque mounted on a machined flat spot. He also chose as foot stone a more modest erratic, with another "Dwight R. Burrell" plaque, so that you would know how he lies, head and foot. Dr. Burrell also contributed a sofa-sized stone lozenge on which a brass plaque commemorating the Canandaigua Treaty of 1794 between the Senecas and the new United States was installed in the early 20th century.

Dr. Burrell's gravestone has grown a lush toupee of moss in its hundred years of use. It grays with the winters and greens up each spring. His only publication in scientific annals that survives to this day is an exposition on a patient who talked eloquently and at length while he was asleep.

Finally, though of course it's by no means final, there is the boy, a Seneca orphan who was one day out hunting. Since he was a boy he was hunting only birds and his scouting had taken him from his village in the valley to a hillside curiously bare of trees. It was lunch time, and he opened his pouch that contained a little acorn meal mixed with maple sugar. He wanted some shade in which to eat and rest, so he tucked himself into the little shadow beside a big standing stone. He'd just begun eating when he heard a voice say, "Would you like to hear a story?"

About the Author

Stephen Lewandowski has published twelve small books of poetry, and his poems and essays have appeared in regional and national environmental and literary journals and anthologies.

He is a graduate of Hamilton College, and he later did graduate work with Louis Jones in the Cooperstown Graduate Programs in American Folk Culture, and later, with Howard Nemerov and William Gass at Washington University in St. Louis.

Lewandowski has worked as an environmental educator and consultant in the western Finger Lakes for thirty-five years. He is a founder of the Coalition for Hemlock and Canadice Lakes, as well as the Canandaigua Lake Watershed Task Force. More recently he has been employed as the Program Director of the Lake Ontario Coastal Initiative

While continuing to write, he has received environmental achievement awards from the Finger Lakes Community College, Canandaigua Lake Pure Waters, Livingston County Environcmtnal Management Council, Western New York Chapter of The Nature Conservancy, and the Finger Lakes Land Trust.

His *O Lucky One* was published by Foothills Publishing in 2010.

Other Recent Titles from Mayapple Press:

Hilma Contreras, Trans. Judith Kerman, *Between Two Silences / Entre Dos Silencios,* 2013
        Paper, 126pp, $16.95; plus s&h
        ISBN 978-1-936419-31-9

Helen Ruggieri & Linda Underhill, Eds., *Writtem on Water: Writings about the Allegheny River,* 2013
        Paper, 108pp, $19.95; includes Bonus CD; plus s&h
        ISBN 978-1-936419-30-2

Don Cellini, *Candidates for sainthood and other sinners / Aprendices de santo y otros pecadores,* 2013
        Paper, 62pp, $14.95 plus s&h
        ISBN 978-1-936419-29-6

Gerry LaFemina, *Notes for the Novice Ventriloquist,* 2013
        Paper, 78pp, $15.95 plus s&h
        ISBN 978-1-936419-28-9

Robert Haight, *Feeding Wild Birds,* 2013
        Paper, 82pp, $15.95 plus s&h
        ISBN 978-1-936419-27-2

Pamela Miller, *Miss Unthinkable,* 2013
        Paper, 58pp, $14.95 plus s&h
        ISBN 978-1-936419-26-5

Penelope Scambly Schott, *Lillie was a goddess, Lillie was a whore,* 2013
        Paper, 90pp, $15.95 plus s&h
        ISBN 978-1-936419-25-8

Nola Garrett, *The Pastor's Wife Considers Pinball,* 2013
        Paper, 74pp, $14.95 plus s&h
        ISBN 978-1-936419-16-6

Marjorie Manwaring, *Search for a Velvet-Lined Cape,* 2013
        Paper, 94pp, $15.95 plus s&h
        ISBN 978-1-936419-15-9

Edythe Haendel Schwartz, *A Palette of Leaves,* 2012
        Paper, 74pp, $14.95 plus s&h
        ISBN 978-1-936419-14-2

Sarah Busse, *Somewhere Piano,* 2012
        Paper, 72pp, $14.95 plus s&h
        ISBN 978-1-936419-13-5

Betsy Johnson-Miller, *Fierce This Falling,* 2012
        Paper, 72pp, $14.95 plus s&h
        ISBN 978-1-936419-12-8

For a complete catalog of Mayapple Press publications, please visit our website at *www. mayapplepress.com.* Books can be ordered direct from our website with secure on-line payment using PayPal, or by mail (check or money order). Or order through your local bookseller.